First Published by Evans Brothers Limited
2A Portman Mansions,Chiltern Street, London W1U 6NR,
United Kingdom

This edition published under license from Evans Brothers
Limited

North America edition published by Chelsea Clubhouse,
a division of Chelsea House Publishers and a subsidiary of
Haights Cross Communications
2080 Cabot Boulevard West, Suite 201, Langhorne,
PA 19047-1813

A Haights Cross Communications ✔ Company

Printed in China

Library of Congress Cataloging-in-Publication Data
applied for.

ISBN 0-7910-8182-6

Acknowledgments

The author and publishers would like to thank the following
for their help with this book:

Aneil, Santosh, and Sanjay Mehta, Aunt Kally, Joshua,
Kieran, Ricky, and Haresh and the rest of the Mehta family.

Thanks also to the Anaphylaxis Campaign for their help in
the preparation of this book.

All photographs by Gareth Boden

Credits

Series Editor: Louise John
Editor: Julia Bird
Designer: Mark Holt
Production: Jenny Mulvanny

LIKE ME LIKE YOU

Aneil Has a
FOOD ALLERGY

JILLIAN POWELL

CHELSEA CLUBHOUSE
An Imprint of Chelsea House Publishers
A Haights Cross Communications Company
Philadelphia

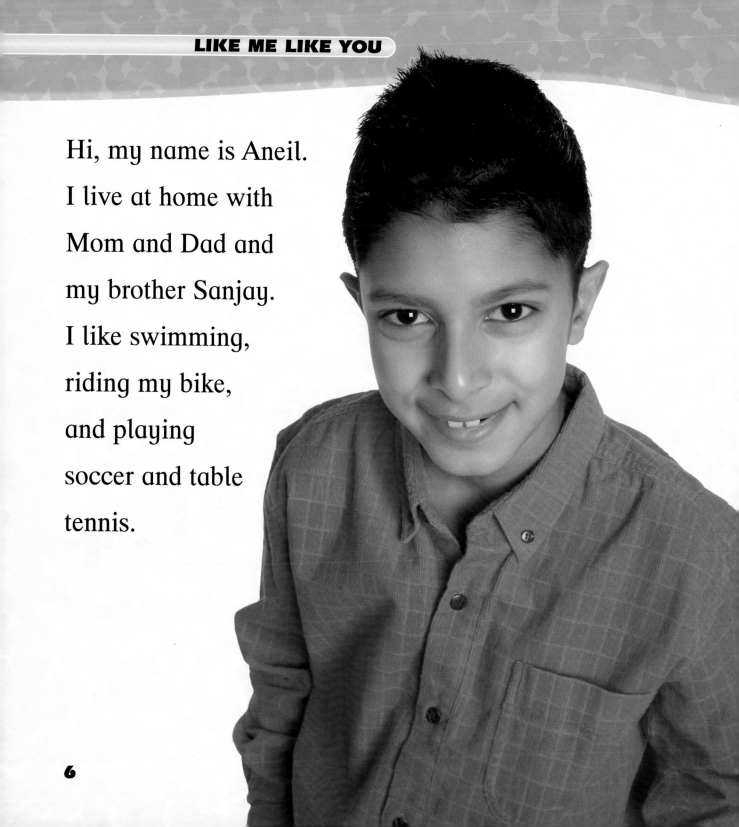

Hi, my name is Aneil.
I live at home with
Mom and Dad and
my brother Sanjay.
I like swimming,
riding my bike,
and playing
soccer and table
tennis.

I have a **food allergy**. If I eat anything containing nuts, they make me ill. Just touching nuts can start my allergy. If Sanjay eats them, he has to wash his hands before coming near me!

FOOD ALLERGY

A **food allergy** is when the body reacts badly to food that is harmless for most people.

7

My family found out I had a food allergy when I was three years old. I ate some nuts and they made me cough. My lips and eyes puffed up and I was sick. They had to take me to hospital to have an **injection** of **adrenaline** to make me better.

Now I have to be very careful not to eat any foods that contain nuts. Breakfast cereals sometimes contain nuts, so Mom and I have to check the labels to make sure I can eat them.

Most food allergies begin in childhood. Some children grow out of allergies, especially to milk or eggs.

Today, we're going to my cousin Kieran's birthday party. Mom is making hot dogs for the party so we need to buy some rolls. Mom asks the baker if there are any nuts or traces of nuts — which means tiny bits of nuts — in the rolls.

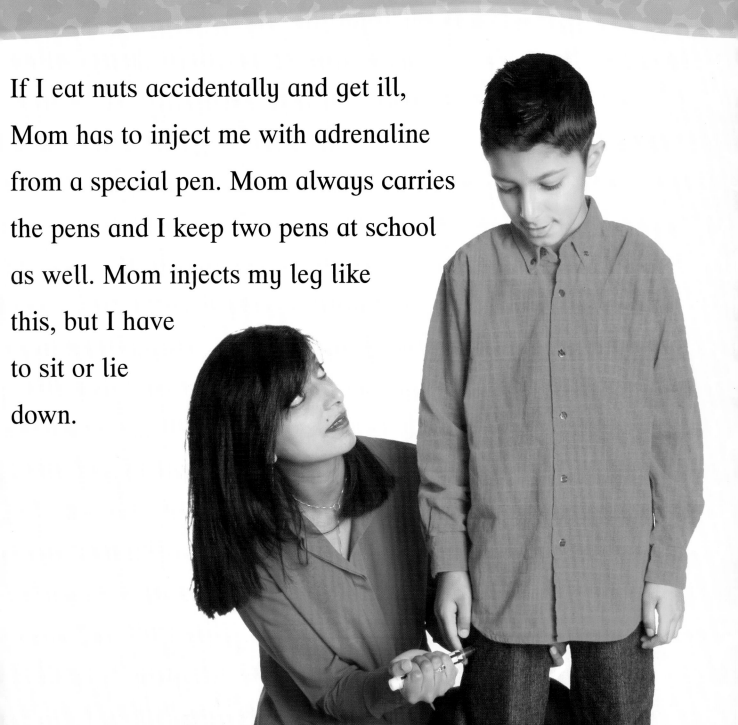

If I eat nuts accidentally and get ill, Mom has to inject me with adrenaline from a special pen. Mom always carries the pens and I keep two pens at school as well. Mom injects my leg like this, but I have to sit or lie down.

Shopping can take a long time, because Mom and I have to check all the food labels. We check to see that there are no nuts or traces of nuts in anything we're buying.

Cakes, cookies, and chocolate can all contain nuts. Lots of other foods can contain traces of nuts. Even foods like ice cream and pasta sauce can contain tiny bits of nuts that could make me ill.

We arrive at Kieran's house early. Mom has brought the hot dogs. She needs to check with Aunt Kally if there is any food at the party that I won't be able to eat because it contains nuts.

I say hello to my cousins Kieran, Haresh, and Ricky and their dog Rex. I would love to have a dog, too, but we can't because animal fur can give me a reaction called **eczema** that makes my skin itch.

OTHER ALLERGIES

Children with food allergies often have other conditions such as **asthma** and **eczema**.

I love ATVs and we always have a great time playing on them at Kieran's house. Rex wants to join in, too!

Mom and Aunt Kally are checking the food in the kitchen. They read all the labels to make sure nothing contains nuts or traces of nuts. They have to check everything, like the rolls for the burgers, cookies, and cake.

I have a big family! My grandpa and grandma are at the party, as well as my mom and dad, aunt and uncle, and cousins. There is lots of food for us to eat.

There are some special Asian dishes like **lentil** curry and ludu, which are candies made from flour, sugar, and milk. Mom reminds me that these dishes might have nuts in them.

I'm sitting next to my friend Joshua. We're in the same class at school. Joshua has food allergies, too. He can't eat the lentil curry because he's allergic to lentils.

The foods that most often cause allergies include milk, eggs, nuts, wheat, fish, shellfish, and soybeans.

Joshua has brought a big birthday present to the party for Kieran. Kieran loves getting presents!

It's time for Kieran to cut the cake! He blows out the candles first. It's a sponge cake. Mom has checked that it has no nuts in it, so it's okay for me to eat.

Aunt Kally is giving Joshua, Sanjay, and me party bags to take home. They have little toys and candies in them. I can't wait to look in mine!

23

It's been a great party but it's time to go home now. We say good-bye to Aunt Kally and to our cousins.

When we get home, Sanjay and I look in our party bags. I got a chocolate bar that might have nuts in it, so Mom tells me to trade with Sanjay. His chocolate bar is safe for me to eat.

The worst thing about having a food allergy is that you can't always eat what everyone else is eating. Sometimes I have to miss a party if we don't know what the food will be like. Mom or Dad will stay at home with me.

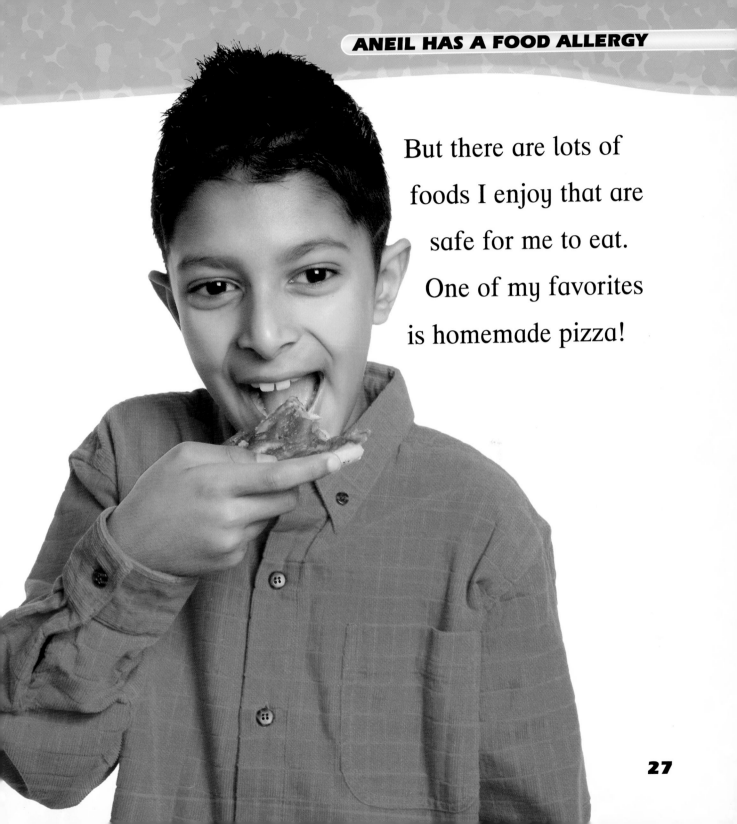

But there are lots of foods I enjoy that are safe for me to eat. One of my favorites is homemade pizza!

Glossary

Adrenaline a medicine that helps to calm allergic reactions, making it easier to breathe

Asthma a condition that causes problems with breathing; it can be an allergy

Eczema a condition that causes a rash and itching; it can be an allergy

Food allergy when the body reacts badly to food that is harmless for most people

Injection having a prick from a needle to put something into our body

Lentil a kind of plant seed that is eaten as a vegetable

Index

Further Information

The Food Allergy and Anaphylaxis Network USA (FAAN)

www.foodallergy.org

Resources and educational information, including links to www.fankids.org—the website of Food Allergy News for Kids. FAAN is dedicated to bringing about a clearer understanding of the issues surrounding food allergies.

Food Allergy News for Kids

www.fankids.org

Areas on this website include: Food Allergy Basics; Tips for Managing Food Allergies; School Project Ideas; and FANKID Clubhouse. Among the activities are label-reading games and word puzzles. The site's mascot is Alexander, the Elephant Who Couldn't Eat Peanuts.

AllergicChild.com

800-444-4094

www.allergicchild.com

Help for children with severe allergies to peanuts, milk, eggs, and soy products.

Parents of Children with Food Allergies Inc.

508-893-6977

www.foodallergykids.org

Provides information and support to families of children with food allergies who need emotional support. Services include a newsletter, conferences, special events, and phone support.

BOOKS

Kid Friendly Allergy Cookbook,
Lynn Rominger, F&W Publications, Inc., 2004

The Complete Idiot's Guide to Food Allergies,
Lee H. Freund, NAL, 2003

No Lobster, Please!: A Story of a Child with a Severe Seafood Allergy, Robyn Rogers,
Heartsome Publishing, 2003

Stories from the Heart: A Collection of Essays by Teens with Food Allergies, vol. 2,
Anne Munoz-Furlong,
Food Allergy & Anaphylaxis Network, 2002